ARCHITECTURE

by Donald J. Canty
Senior Editor, *Architectural Forum* magazine

Thanks are due to the American Institute of
Architects, Washington, D. C., for assistance in
preparing the requirements and pamphlet for the
Architecture merit badge.

BOY SCOUTS OF AMERICA
IRVING, TEXAS

**1990 Printing of the
1966 Edition**

REQUIREMENTS

1. Write about a period of history that influenced architecture. Compare the buildings of that time with those in the United States today.

2. Write about a building you admire. Describe its arrangement, exterior, interior, and surroundings. Give the function for which the building was designed.

3. Make a sketch of a building you admire (other than the one in requirement 2).

4. Measure a building. Make a drawing of it at a scale of ¼ inch equal to 1 foot. Make one plan and one detail such as a doorway or window. It may be in pencil on tracing or drawing paper. Use simple architectural letters.

CONTENTS

ARCHITECTURE

Copyright 1966
Boy Scouts of America
Irving, Texas
ISBN 0-8395-3321-7
No. 3321   Printed in U.S.A.   3.5M190

INTRODUCTION

Architecture is the setting for our lives. We live in architecture, work in it, learn in it, play in it, are entertained in it, and worship in it. Whenever we walk down a city street—any city street—we are surrounded by architecture on all sides.

We seldom think of our house, our apartment building, our school, or our recreation center as architecture, although we may think of a big office building or a spacious church that way. And yet, small buildings as well as large, simple buildings as well as those that are rich with ornament, all are examples of architecture. They all require the application of that wide range of differing skills and talents which are the architect's.

Someone must conceive how the building is to look and function, then put that concept on paper in the form of sketches and plans. Someone must direct and coordinate the work of all those engaged in the process of building—the draftsmen, the engineers, the contractors, the suppliers of materials and equipment, and the workmen. That someone is the architect. This booklet is about him and his profession.

ARCHITECTURE
ITS HISTORY

Architecture in our time is an expression of two basic freedoms. One is a freedom of means. The architect today has at his disposal a range of materials and construction techniques broad enough to build to any size and in any shape he chooses, within the limitations of the project at hand.

This is something completely new. The history of architecture, in part, is a history of men making do with the materials close at hand and with ways of building that changed slowly over centuries. Examples of man's growth in this field are shown on the next few pages.

The massiveness and solidity of the Egyptian pyramids and temples, the first monuments of this history, were much like the

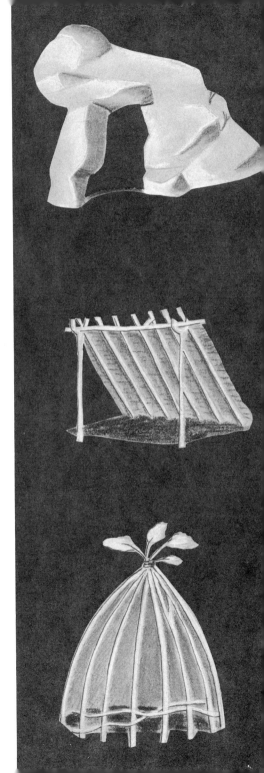

compound dwellings made by the people from bricks baked from the clay of their arid land.

The Greeks had plentiful supplies of granite and marble and used them to fashion noble columns shaped to make the most of sparkling sun and shadow. These columns, which the Greeks placed close together to support heavy roof beams, were enthusiastically borrowed by the Romans.

The Romans also took the arch, the vault, and the dome from earlier civilizations. Combining these devices, they built an empire of stone — stone used in huge blocks or broken up and mixed with cement to form concrete.

After the fall of this empire and the centuries that followed, Romanesque architecture took up where the Romans had left off. This transition occurred for a very good reason — the ruins of the Roman buildings on all sides contained vast quantities of usable fragments.

This brings us to the second aspect of the freedom enjoyed by

Shea Stadium

Progressive Retail Store

today's architects — the nearly complete freedom from the past. This, too, is entirely new; for, from the Middle Ages to the present century, the history of architecture has been a story of the reuse, the modification, and the elaboration of previous styles.

Thus, the Gothic era which produced the magnificent cathedrals of Europe began with the point-ing of the top of the rounded Romanesque arch, then the piling of stones closer to the heavens in delicate feats of structural balance.

The Renaissance brought an explosion of combinations of past devices—Gothic methods of construction, Greek and Roman columns and ornamentation, even Byzantine domes from the East —with such dazzling results as St. Peter's in Rome.

Renaissance architecture became Baroque with the casting off of restraint in form and ornamentation.

This piecing together of past styles with a mortar of new ideas continued to be the accepted way to practice architecture until a few decades ago. It was unthinkable that a building would be designed without some recognizable borrowing from an earlier era, and the borrowing often went all the way back to the Greeks. Then came the so-called modern movement, the most sudden and sweeping revolution architecture has experienced.

Empire State Building

United Nations Buildings

Huntington Hartford
Gallery of Modern Art

The revolution was partly technological. Iron and steel were developed and proved for structural use, and new metals like aluminum came into being. The potentialities of concrete were explored and expanded almost for the first time since Roman days. Glass was refined and made more widely available, thus changing the entire relationship between the interior of buildings and the world outside.

Mass production and improved methods of transportation and distribution began to lessen the architect's dependence on the materials that could be cut from

9

forests or carved from the earth close at hand. And engineering began the headlong rush of discovery that has continued to the present day.

This architectural revolution has produced such modern buildings as Shea Stadium, the Empire State Building, the United Nations buildings, and countless other office buildings, civic centers, and homes of the type shown in this pamphlet.

The revolution was also partly economic. Great cities that had been founded originally as the marketing centers of the nation and as seats of state and church became centers of industry, commerce, and communication. The people flocked to them from the land.

Higher buildings were needed than had ever been seen before. These buildings were commissioned by industrialists and managers, rather than by bishops and princes. They were practical buildings that served the new demands for efficiency. Labor demanded and got a larger share of the output of business and industry, and the cost of elaborate handcrafted ornamentation be-

Police Administration Building, Philadelphia, Pa.

came prohibitive.

But this revolution, like others, was primarily one of ideas. Architects looked at the world about them and saw that the buildings of the past were no longer suitable. They saw what the new materials and technology offered.

Pioneers like Louis Sullivan, Frank Lloyd Wright, Le Corbusier, Walter Gropius, and Mies van der Rohe provided the examples of a new approach in buildings. While dating from the 1920's and earlier, their buildings look as though they might have been built today. Their idea was that architects should forget the past and look to the problems and promise of the present. They urged architects to disdain ornament and let beauty grow from the way a building is constructed and the way it is shaped to serve its function.

These revolutionary ideas, born before World War I, took hold of the architectural profession in the ensuing 20 years and came into general use after World War II. Today, as is the case with most successful revolutions, there are some second

thoughts about it. Were some past ideas—as opposed to past styles — perhaps discarded too hastily? Has the new freedom which architects enjoy led to the overemphasis of novelty? Should the revolution now enter a new phase to prepare the profession of architecture for the present era of even more rapid technological advancement and population growth?

Whatever the answers to such questions, it is clear that the modern movement as shown by the buildings on pages 6-13 has worked a permanent change—not just in the way buildings look,

Today's Private Home

but in the way architecture is practiced.

Nearly any moment in architecture's past can be fascinating and fruitful to study in detail, and can put new light on the present and future.

Contemporary Church

Assembly Building, Chandigarh, India

13

ARCHITECTURE ITS MEANING

The building at left, Yale University's School of Arts and Architecture, is one of the most recent works of architecture in America. What about it is so different from many other buildings? Before you choose a building to describe, let's take a close look.

The photos and sketches of this building, shown on the next few pages, should help you learn the meaning of architecture.

To find the answers, we will take a word and picture tour of the building with its architect guiding us part of the way. But first, let's consider some of the qualities by which architects judge their work:

Function is the way the building does its job—the way it fits the uses for which it was built. If a building does not function well, it cannot be a great work of architecture, no matter how beautiful it may seem.

15

Suitability to surroundings is the way the building blends into its street and neighborhood. This is especially important if the neighborhood has a strong character, a strong feeling about it, as in the case of the Yale campus.

Suitability to site is the way the building makes use of the natural characteristics of the land on which it rises. This becomes a key factor if the site is hilly or irregular in shape, or if it contains beautiful rocks or trees. "The good building," said the late Frank Lloyd Wright, America's most famous architect, "is one that makes the landscape more beautiful than it was before."

Form is basically the shape the building takes, but it is hard to separate it from the two qualities described above. One key element of the building's form is its *massing*—the way the bulk of one wing of the building is played off against the other, for example. Another is its *silhouette,* the outline the building makes against the sky. Still another is its *proportions,* the way one element of the building relates in size and shape to others. And finally there is *scale,* the way the building and its parts relate in size to the people who will use it, to the activities that will go on inside, and to the buildings and features of the landscape.

Surface is determined by the materials that go into the building, its colors, and its textures. An important factor here, and one that has a great impact on the building's form, is the way the architect uses light and shadow to enrich the walls or alternates solid walls with openness or windows.

Space is simply the quality of the building's interiors. Space is invisible and intangible. In a work of architecture like a great high-ceilinged cathedral, it is

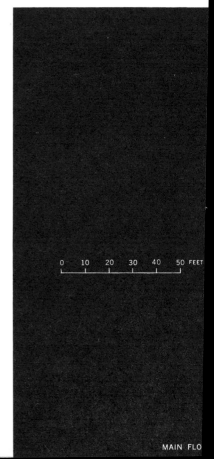

MAIN FLO

space that creates the sense of awe and reverence you feel so strongly when you enter. Space has been called the basic raw material of architecture. Building is, after all, simply the process of enclosing and controlling space.

Environment is the way space is controlled to accommodate whatever goes on inside the building. It has to do with the use of natural and artificial light, temperature, humidity, the flow of air, and acoustics, the quality of sound in the building.

Top View

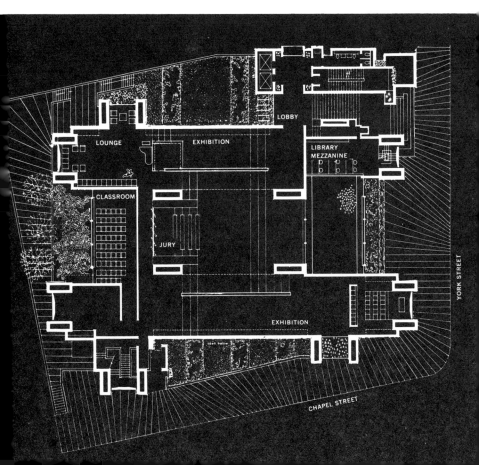

CUTAWAY VIEW FROM CHAPEL STREET

1. SCULPTURE STUDIO
2. LECTURE HALL
3. MECHANICAL
4. DARKROOMS
5. LIBRARY
6. MAIN HALL & "JURY PIT"
7. CLASSROOM
8. FACULTY OFFICES
9. DRAFTING ROOM
10. PAINTING STUDIOS
11. STORAGE

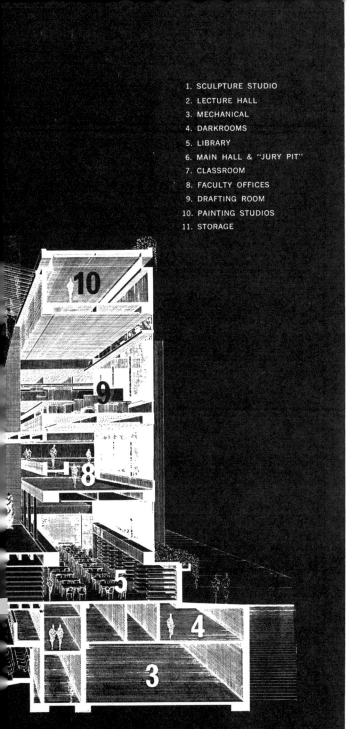

Architect's Sketches

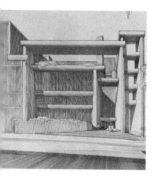

With these things in mind, we can try to look at the Yale building the way an architect would.

Any large building, as we shall see, grows in the mind of its architect before it grows at its site. The architect of the Yale building was Paul Rudolph, who is dean of the School of Arts and Architecture (putting him in the unusual position of being, in part, his own client). Mr. Rudolph studied six different approaches to the design of the building before he settled on the final one. Two of the early studies are shown at left, and the finished building on page 22.

Mr. Rudolph's first concern was the building's surroundings. Its site was a corner at one edge of the Yale campus. From the beginning, he says, "There was always the notion that this was a building that turned the corner." It was to be a gateway leading into the heart of the campus. The photograph shows how the massive towers lead the eye around the corner. The building seems almost to be in motion.

Its most striking aspects, in fact, are rhythm and irregularity (and, of course, strength). Mr. Rudolph has taken the opposite approach to that of the classical architects with their fondness for balance and symmetry. Here the walls pop in and out, the towers vary in height, and nothing comes out quite even. And all these changes and surprises in the building's outside form reflect even greater freedom inside.

The way a building functions, the way it does the job for which it was intended, is usually best shown in a *plan drawing*, like the one on pages 18 and 19. But the Yale Arts and Architecture Building is an unusually complicated building, with a whole complicated list of jobs to do. It has to provide classrooms and lecture halls, drafting rooms for the architectural students, studios for the students of painting and sculpture, a library, offices for faculty members, and so on. And beyond these things, Mr. Rudolph had still another function in mind for the building; it should help teach the students of architecture something about drama and variety in the use of space.

The end result was that the building wound up with 36 different levels by Mr. Rudolph's own count. The way it works thus has to be shown in a cutaway view as well as a plan drawing.

The building is, to begin with, bigger than it looks from outside. There are two full floors below the level of the street. From street level on up, the smaller rooms are placed around the

edges of two large spaces in the middle. One is a large exhibit hall with a "pit" where critical juries review students' work; the other, above the exhibit hall, is the drafting room. Visitors go through a constantly changing series of experiences as they walk around the building, but glimpses of these two big central rooms keep them from getting lost.

An architectural critic visiting the building for the first time described his experiences this way: "Floors step up and down. Ceilings soar or suddenly descend near head level. Each room seems as if it had been invented as a new kind of space."

Some of what he felt is shown in the pictures on these pages. The library on page 25, for example, has a low ceiling over the stacks of books and the magazine racks but opens to a two-story room whose upper reaches are windows looking into the exhibit hall. Or take the huge

23

Drafting Room

Library

drafting room. Some tables are on balconies. These balconies are supported by immense cross-beams between even larger columns but have ceilings only 7 feet high. Yet, other tables are in the area below in a volume that has the dimensions of a great church.

"Everywhere, everywhere, everywhere there should be something to see," says Mr. Rudolph, and everywhere inside the Arts and Architecture Building there are eye-filling images. Sometimes they are glimpses of the outdoors let in by the irregularly placed windows. Sometimes they are surprising objects like a section of ornament from a noble building of the past. Sometimes they are works of art, from modern paintings to ancient statues like the one in the photograph above. And sometimes they are simply the play of surfaces of the building itself.

Yale University's buildings are mostly of stone, rugged and weathered. Mr. Rudolph used concrete to give the surface of the Arts and Architecture Building something of the same look. The concrete was poured in specially made forms that gave it vertical stripes of sharp-edged ridges. Workmen then went over the building inch by inch, hammering the edges off by hand. The result is a rough, corduroy-like texture that contrasts with the metal and glass of the windows and with the smooth-surfaced concrete used for trim as shown on pages 26 and 27.

The final test of the building

is the way all of its parts come together — the spaces shaped by the job the building has to do, the form expressing the variety of the inside spaces, and the rough surface reinforcing the rhythmic strength of the form. It is this kind of unity that makes a building a work of architecture.

Now it's your turn to describe a building of your choice. Select it with care, if possible with the help of your counselor. The description should answer questions like these: How many floors does the building have? What are the principal materials used, inside and out? What is the general shape of the building from the outside? Are there any especially impressive features or details that immediately catch the eye? Inside, do you get any special feeling from the ways that space is handled? Does the layout seem logical and efficient?

In other words, first give the facts about the building. Then give your impressions of it, trying to look at it the way an architect would see it.

ARCHITECTURE
ITS DESIGN

The architect's best means of communication is his drawing pencil. Design ideas must be shown rather than described in words. Drawings are the tools by which the architect shows the client what the building will be like; they are the tools by which he tells the contractors and workmen how it is to be built. It is probably best, as a beginning, to use a soft (but not smudgy) pencil and an informal technique. Try to convey the general impression of what the building looks like, as shown below, instead of precisely rendering each detail. A head-on view is easiest as a start. A perspective view—the way the building looks from an angle — is more difficult, but you might want to try one with the advice of your counselor.

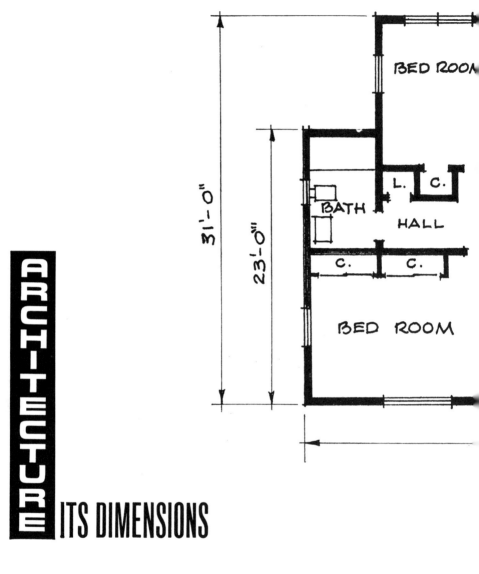

ARCHITECTURE
ITS DIMENSIONS

The measurement of rooms is painstaking work but it has an important purpose. An architect must be able to visualize the way various dimensions will look and feel in the finished building. He obviously can't make a full-scale mockup of every element to see how it will turn out. Measuring is a way to develop this ability to visualize. Also, the architect's

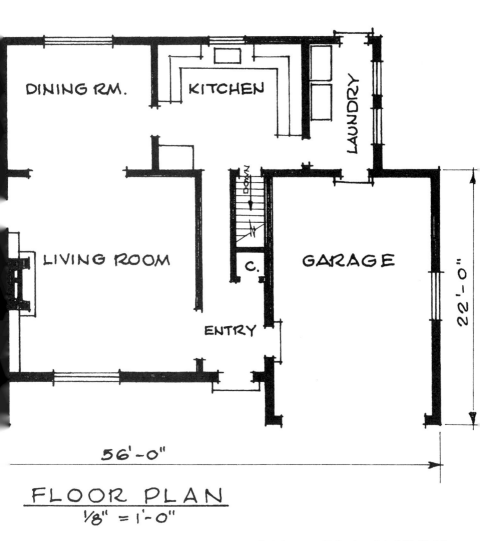

FLOOR PLAN
1/8" = 1'-0"

RESIDENCE FOR: WILLIAM BROWN, SR.
LOCATION: FREEHOLD, NEW JERSEY
DATE DRAWN: JUNE 10, 1965
DRAWN BY: CHARLES BEACH

plans and specifications must be exact down to the last fraction of an inch. Measuring teaches this kind of precision.

In drawing the floor plan, consult your counselor (or any standard architectural textbook) for the accepted symbols to use in designating windows, doors, and other elements. Follow the illustration above for ideas.

ARCHITECTURE ITS PRACTICE

There is a story behind every work of architecture. It is a story of dreams, wishes, artistry, and inspiration. It is also a story of endless details, decisions, complicated problems, choices, and plain hard work.

The cast of characters is a long one—engineers, draftsmen, building suppliers, inspectors, contractors, and workmen. But only two people (or groups of people) appear in every chapter. They are the architect and his client.

It is the architect's job to guide every step of the process

of creating a building. He acts as the client's agent. He enters the process even before the land is selected and before the client is quite sure exactly what kind of a building he wants. His work can continue even after the building is completed and the client moves in.

What the architect does along the way can be told most clearly in the story of a house.

The story begins with the decision of the clients, a young couple, to build. They have a set amount of money they can spend, an idea of where they would like to live, and some general notions of the kind of house they want. They talk to several architects, look at some of their work, and finally choose the one they feel can do the best job.

Next, they go looking for a lot with the architect along. The way the lot faces, the prevailing winds, the number and kinds of trees, the stability of the soil, and the contours of the ground are all things that will help shape the house.

As possible sites are inspected, decisions that will affect the design are being made — decisions

about the relationship between the house and its grounds, about the importance of views, about whether the house should be compact or rambling in its layout.

When the lot is selected the process of design begins in earnest. Before pencil touches paper, however, the architect must learn a good deal about the couple. He must try to get a clear idea of the way they like to live, their likes and dislikes, and their present and future needs. Some requirements they state immediately but others he must draw out of them with the skill and knowledge of a psychologist.

The architect comes out of these conversations with a program for the house—a statement, either written or in his mind, of what needs and desires the house should satisfy. Working from this program, from the nature of the site, and within the limitations of the budget, he then begins to draw preliminary plans and sketches. These propose a general layout for the house, the shape it might take, and the principal materials to be used.

He shows his clients these preliminary drawings and another round of discussions begins. An

architect develops the ability to think in visual terms, so that even during the earlier talks the ideas discussed were becoming images in his mind. For the clients, however, the preliminary drawings contain the first real idea of what their house might be. They go over them eagerly and critically, questioning some of the architect's proposals and enthusiastically accepting others.

The architect revises the drawings, changing some aspects of the design and making others more specific. Gradually he and his clients come to agree on what every room, every wall, and every window should be like. They look at samples of materials, swatches of colors, and items of equipment. They may consult engineers on the structure of the house, the heating and air conditioning system, or the lighting. The clients approve the preliminary drawings—and the most time-consuming part of the architect's job begins.

The architect's and clients' concept of the house must be communicated to those who will actually do the work of con-

struction. This is done through working drawings and specifications, which the architect now prepares. The working drawings — the blueprints, as they are often called—must show the design, the location, and the size of every part of the building. They include plans, elevations that show the walls head on, sections that slice the house open at various points, and crucial details. The specifications describe, in words, every item that goes into the house. They tell how it is to be put in place and state the standards of quality that will be applied to the workmanship.

These drawings and specifications are painstaking work for the architect and his staff. When they are finished, they are a complete and precise description of what the house is to be like and how it is to be built. They are the basis of the contractors' bids and for all the work of building the new home.

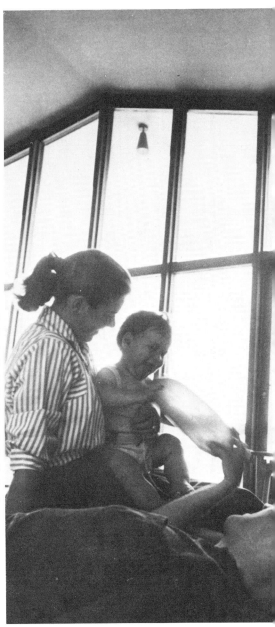

The architect's next task is to see that they are followed so that the house is built as designed. He inspects the job at crucial stages of construction and approves payments to the contractors only after each part of the house is properly completed. Then, one day months after he first met his clients, he calls to tell them that the last part of the job is finished. The house is theirs to use and enjoy.

At the beginning of a new project the architect must be an investigator, ferreting out the clients' needs and tastes. Then he must be a diagnostician, isolating and defining the problems to be solved. Next he becomes the planner organizing space, circulation, and facilities to meet the clients' requirements. Then he is the creator seeking to

ARCHITECTURE THE MAN

produce an original and satisfying work of art.

From this point on he is the coordinator directing the work of hosts of others from engineers to workmen. He is also an agent **representing the clients'** interests in the purchase and use of goods and services. During construction he is, to some degree, a policeman, but he is also an arbitrator of disputes between the clients and the contractors.

And always, the architect must be enough of a businessman to keep his practice going and meet his office payroll.

The architect, then, is expected to have a great many qualities normally considered to be opposites: creativeness and practicality, imagination and prudence, individuality and group leadership, sensitivity and business acumen. He is part administrator, **part** constructor, part engineer, and part artist. To be sure, large architectural firms usually have specialists handling the various parts of the process but the men at the top must be knowledgeable about all of them.

Most architects start with houses and, as their practices grow, they branch out into other, larger kinds of buildings — like the ones shown on these pages. The basic process stays the same —program analysis, design, production of working drawings and specifications, and the overseeing of construction—but every step gets more complex as the size of the project at hand increases.

Take the programing phase, using a hospital as an example. A large hospital is almost a city in itself with a staff of highly trained and specialized people working together in intricate patterns. It can be quite literally a matter of life and death for the architect to understand the workings of the hospital well enough to work out the plan and placement of facilities for maximum efficiency. But the architect's clients are the hospital's patients as well as its staff. He must also create a cheerful, comfortable environment that will speed rather than hinder the healing function of the hospital. So complicated are the hospital's program requirements that some architects are experimenting with the use of electronic computers to plot them.

The situation is the same in the design of a factory, a laboratory, a school, and any number of other building types. Each gets the architect into a new field—into industrial production, scientific research, education — which he must comprehend in order to serve. It is one of the fascinations of his profession, but it is also one of his most demanding challenges.

Or take the preliminary design phase, again using a hospital as an example. The hospital today is virtually a machine, filled with highly sophisticated equipment. It takes massive and flexible installations of electrical, heating, plumbing, air conditioning, ventilating, and power systems to keep this equipment going. (Sometimes, in fact, these systems can account for more than half the total building cost.) The architect cannot be expert in the engineering of each one, but he must know enough about them to mesh their design with the design of the building as a whole. He must be able to coordinate the work of the specialists he calls in for collaboration.

On a large project, in fact, coordination becomes one of the architect's most formidable tasks. He must coordinate first of all the work of his own staff—designers, draftsmen, job captains, specifications writers, and so on down to secretaries and office boys. He must coordinate the work of his consultants — structural, mechanical, electrical, and acoustical engineers; landscape architects; interior decorators; and sometimes others. And he must often coordinate the work of a raft of specialty contractors when construction begins.

Yet, with all this to think about, the architect today is preparing himself to take on even greater responsibilities in the coming decades.

ARCHITECTURE
ITS FUTURE

So far we have twice seen the word "environment." It means our surroundings — the walls around us, the air we breathe, the light and shadows we see, the surfaces we walk on, and the spaces we inhabit. It is the basic concern of architecture.

But architects have come to realize the limited importance of the environment of single buildings. The impact of some of our

greatest buildings — the feelings of awe, satisfaction, and inspiration they generate—disappears as one leaves them and walks down nearby streets designed by everyone and no one. The order and beauty of an individual work of architecture is nearly always surrounded by the mess and jumble we have allowed to spread over much of our cities.

In the next decade millions more people will have come to live in America's urban centers. The problems of blight, decay, overcrowding, and congestion will grow beyond our present fears unless something is done in the meantime. The cores of American cities must be renewed and reordered to again become an environment that will be stimulating rather than smothering. New patterns of us-

ing the remaining land in our metropolitan areas must be found to avoid the sprawl and wastefulness of our present suburbs.

This is the challenge to architecture. It must expand its concern to larger pieces of the urban environment and expand its processes to meet the prospect of a new scale of practice. It may bring to architecture another revolution of thought and method; it is certain to bring to architecture an unprecedented significance and meaning.

BOOKS ABOUT ARCHITECTURE

Recommended by the American Library Association, Advisory Committee to Scouting.

SCOUT LITERATURE

Drafting merit badge pamphlet, 1965.

OTHER BOOKS

All the Ways of Building, L. Lamprey, 1933, 1958.
History of building including social and cultural aspects.

First Book of Architecture, The, Lamont Moore, 1961.
Worldwide examples of architecture arranged by their function: worship, living, earning, governing, pleasure, and learning. Photographs.

First Book of Mechanical Drawing, The, Jerome S. Meyer, 1963.
Explains clearly basic concepts: use of drafting tools, drawing to scale, floor plans, perspective, and architectural lettering.

First Book of Palaces, The, Barbara L. Beck, 1964.
Brief description and sketches of 30 worldwide historical palaces.

From Stones to Skyscrapers: A Book About Architecture, Thea and Richard Bergere, 1960.
Surveys world architecture from prehistoric to contemporary times. Sketches of characteristic details and representative buildings. Useful glossary.

Observer's Book of Architecture, The, John Penoyre, 1961.
Architecture in Britain from the 7th to the 20th century, with numerous explanatory sketches and diagrams in both text and index.